GOVERNMENT AND COMMUNITY

by Marne Ventura

Cody Koala

An Imprint of Pop!

popbooksonline.com

abdopublishing.com

Published by Pop!, a division of ABDO, PO Box 398166, Minneapolis, Minnesota 55439. Copyright © 2019 by POP, LLC. International copyrights reserved in all countries. No part of this book may be reproduced in any form without written permission from the publisher. Pop!™ is a trademark and logo of POP, LLC.

Printed in the United States of America, North Mankato, Minnesota

032018
092018

THIS BOOK CONTAINS RECYCLED MATERIALS

Cover Photo: iStockphoto
Interior Photos: iStockphoto, 1, 5 (top), 5 (bottom right), 6, 14, 17, 19, 20 (top right), 20 (middle right); Shutterstock Images, 5 (bottom left), 9, 10, 13, 20 (top left), 20 (middle left), 20 (bottom left), 20 (bottom right)

Editor: Charly Haley
Series Designer: Laura Mitchell

Library of Congress Control Number: 2017963371

Publisher's Cataloging-in-Publication Data

Names: Ventura, Marne, author.
Title: Government and community / by Marne Ventura.
Description: Minneapolis, Minnesota : Pop!, 2019. | Series: Community economics | Includes online resources and index.
Identifiers: ISBN 9781532160035 (lib.bdg.) | ISBN 9781532161155 (ebook) |
Subjects: LCSH: Local government--Juvenile literature. | Community development--Juvenile literature. | Regional economics--Juvenile literature. | Economic development--Juvenile literature. | Community life--Juvenile literature.
Classification: DDC 330.9--dc23

Hello! My name is

Cody Koala

Pop open this book and you'll find QR codes like this one, loaded with information, so you can learn even more!

Scan this code* and others like it while you read, or visit the website below to make this book pop.

popbooksonline.com/
government-and-community

*Scanning QR codes requires a web-enabled smart device with a QR code reader app and a camera.

Table of Contents

Chapter 1

Community

A community is a place where people live, work, and play. A big city is a community. A small town is a community.

Watch a video here!

People in a community share **services**. They travel on roads and sidewalks.

They play in parks. They call the police or firefighters when they need help.

Towns, cities, and neighborhoods are all examples of communities.

Chapter 2

Government

Many of those services come from the **government**. People in a community **vote** for leaders to run their government.

Learn more here!

The government makes
rules for a community.
Those rules are called laws.

The government also decides how to spend money in the community.

Government meetings are often **public**. People can watch the meetings and talk to leaders.

Chapter 3

Taxes

When people earn money, they pay some of it to the government. This is called paying **taxes**.

People earn
money at work.

Learn more here!

Tax money pays for services such as schools, parks, roads, and libraries. Tax money sometimes helps people who can't pay for food or a place to live.

Taxes also pay government leaders, police officers, firefighters, teachers, and librarians for their work.

Chapter 4

Voting and Elections

People vote for their government leaders in an **election**. The person with the most votes wins the election and becomes a government leader.

Complete an
activity here!

Who works in government?

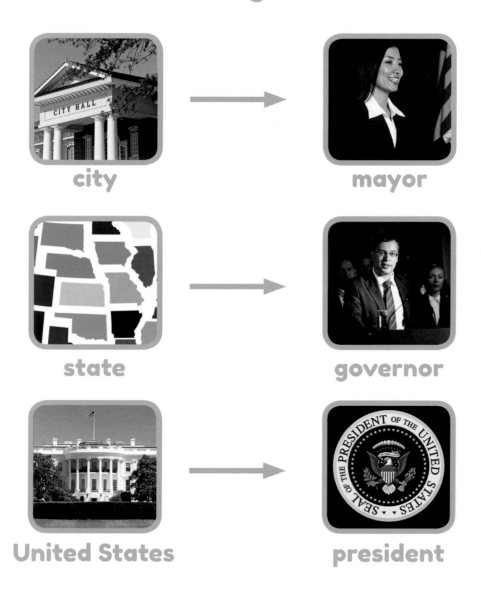

city → mayor

state → governor

United States → president

There are many different leaders in government. City Council members help a mayor run a city. School Board members make rules about schools.

In a city, people elect a mayor as their leader. For the whole United States, people elect a president.

Making Connections

Text-to-Self

Which community services do you use?

Text-to-Text

What are the names of some communities in your favorite books?

Text-to-World

If you were a government leader, what would you do to help your community?

Glossary

election – when people vote for a government leader.

government – the people who run a community.

public – open to all people.

service – work done to help someone.

tax – money that people pay to the government for public purposes.

vote – when a person offers their choice in an election.

Index

Online Resources

popbooksonline.com

Thanks for reading this Cody Koala book!

Scan this code* and others like it in this book, or visit the website below to make this book pop!

popbooksonline.com/government-and-community

*Scanning QR codes requires a web-enabled smart device with a QR code reader app and a camera.